@papeteriebleu

Papeterie Bleu

Shop our other books at
www.pbleu.com

Wholesale distribution through Ingram Content Group
www.ingramcontent.com/publishers/distribution/wholesale

For questions and customer service, email us at
support@pbleu.com

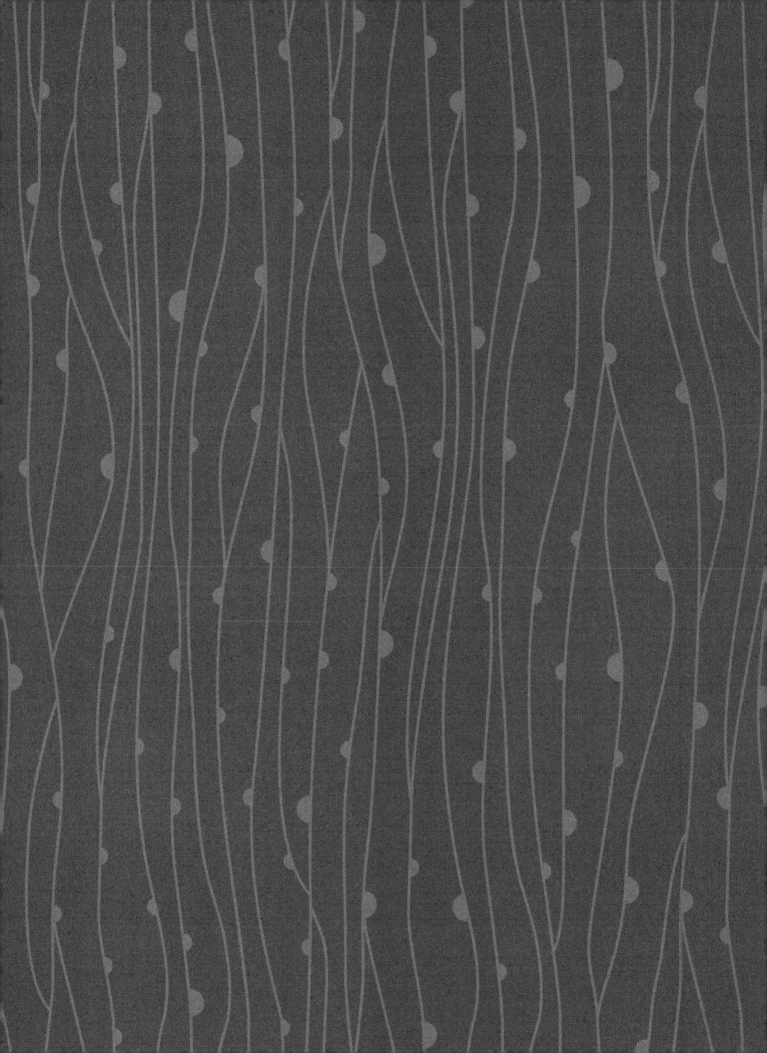

ARGUING WITH A PARALEGAL IS LIKE WRESTLING IN THE MUD WITH A PIG... SOONER OR LATER YOU REALIZE HE PARALEGAL LIKES IT

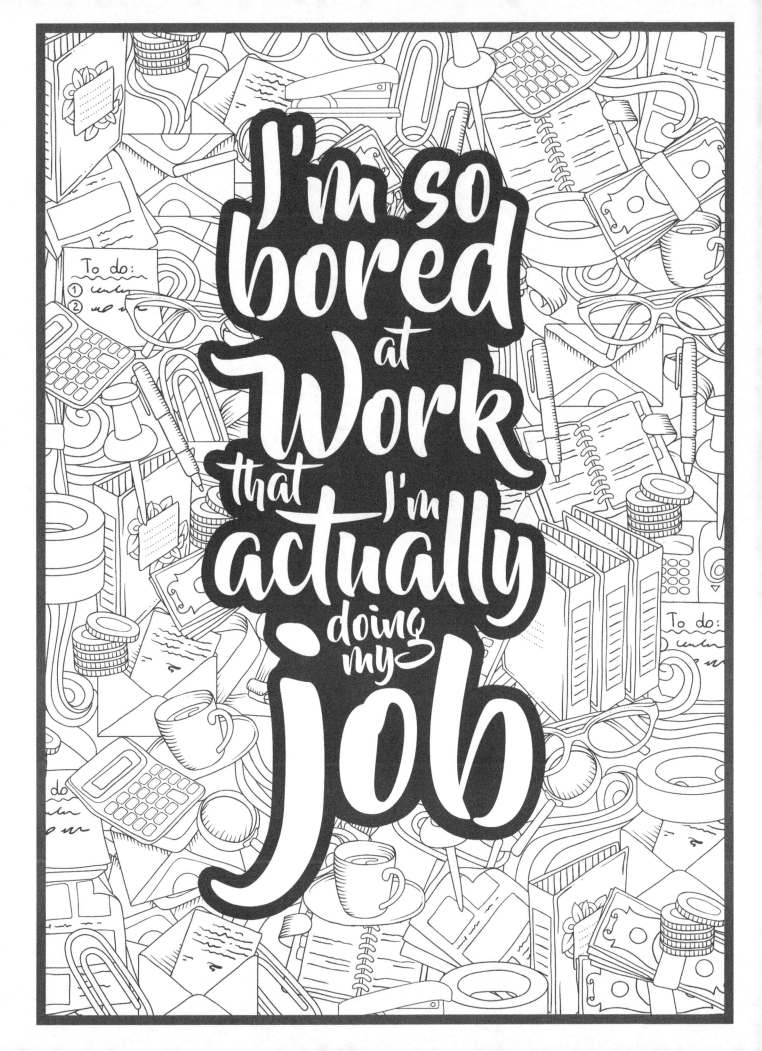

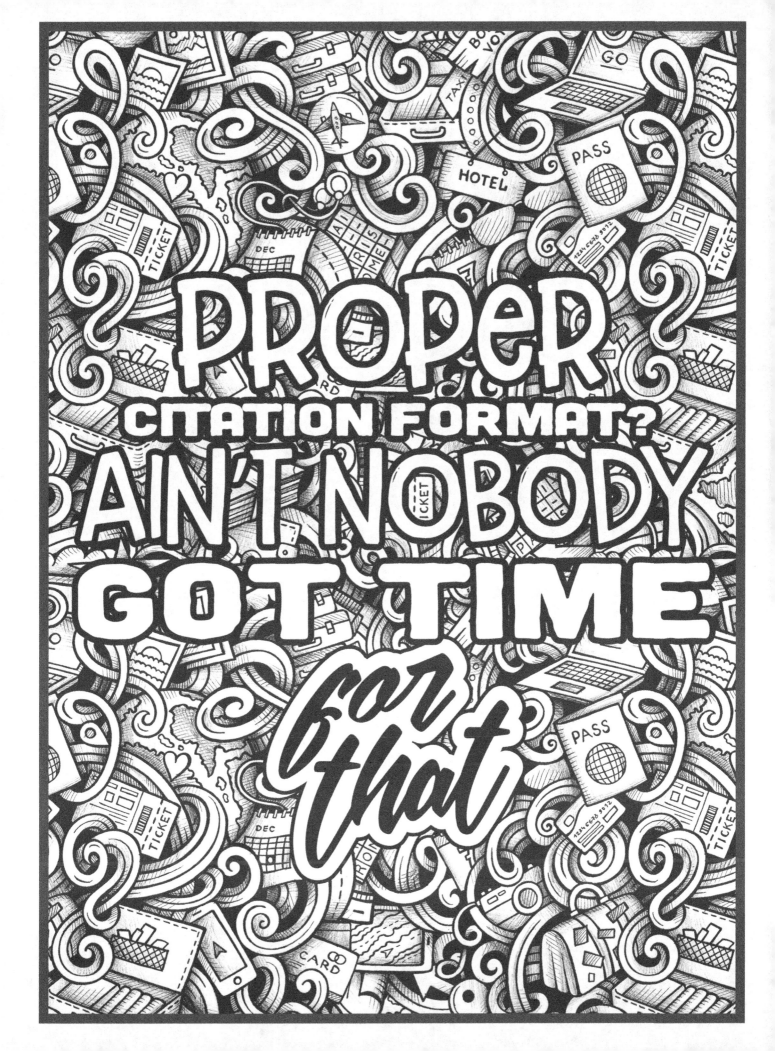

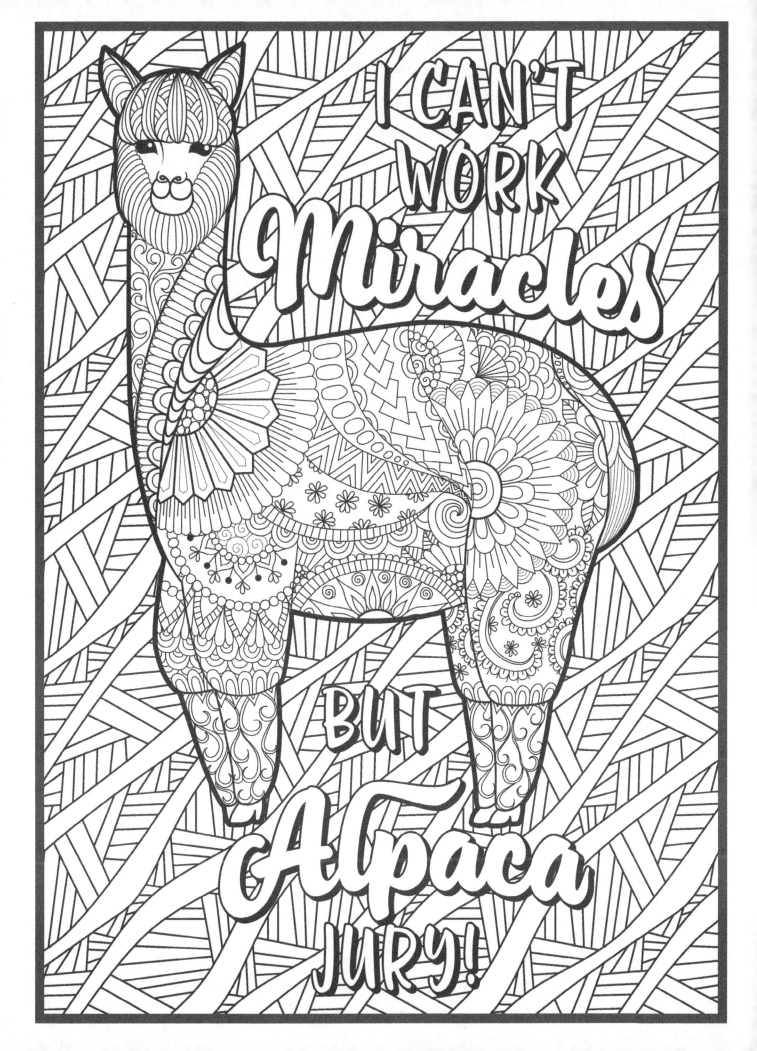

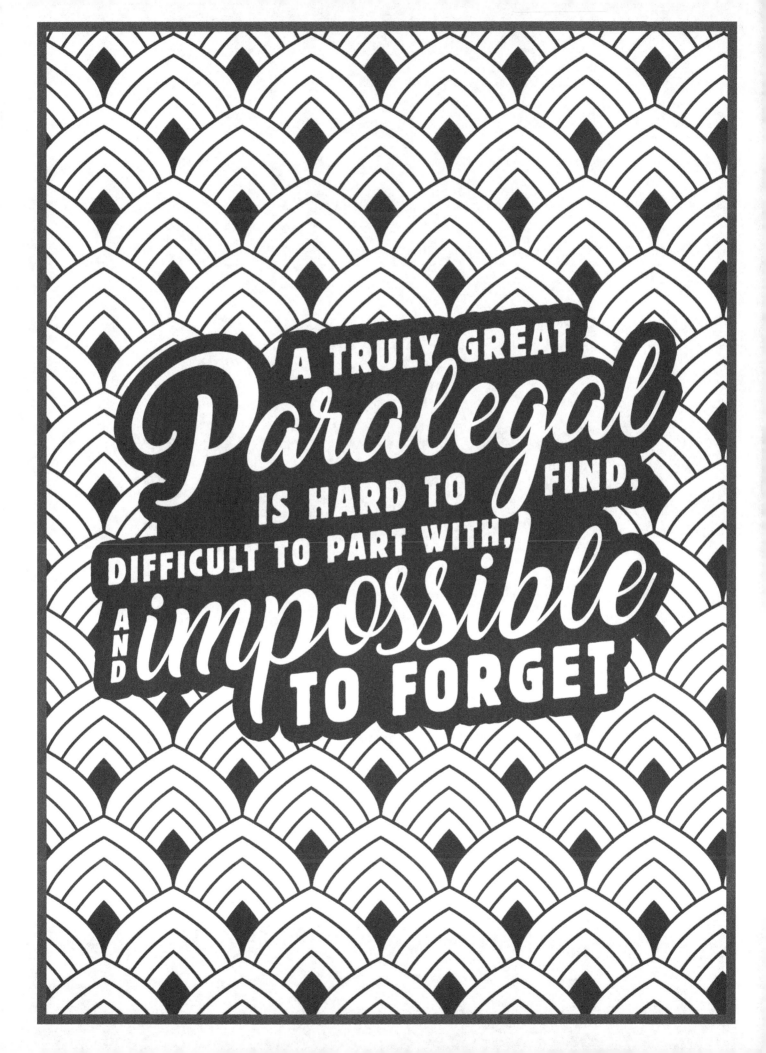

PARALEGAL

LIKE A SUPER HERO.

ONLY REAL

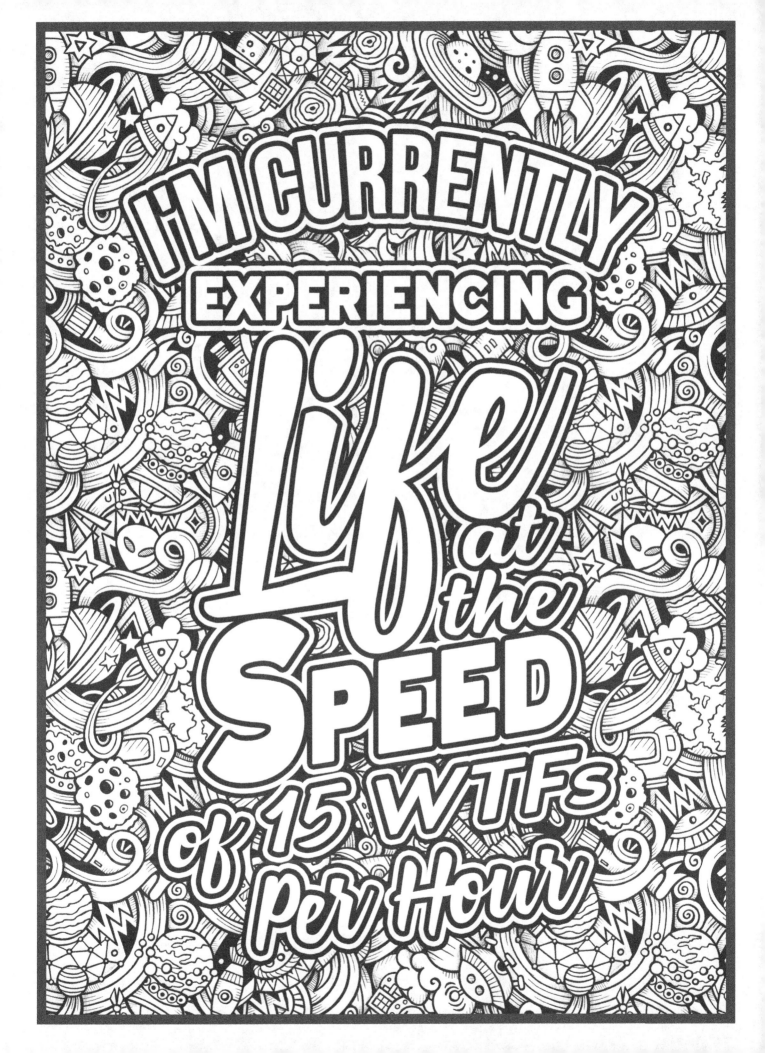

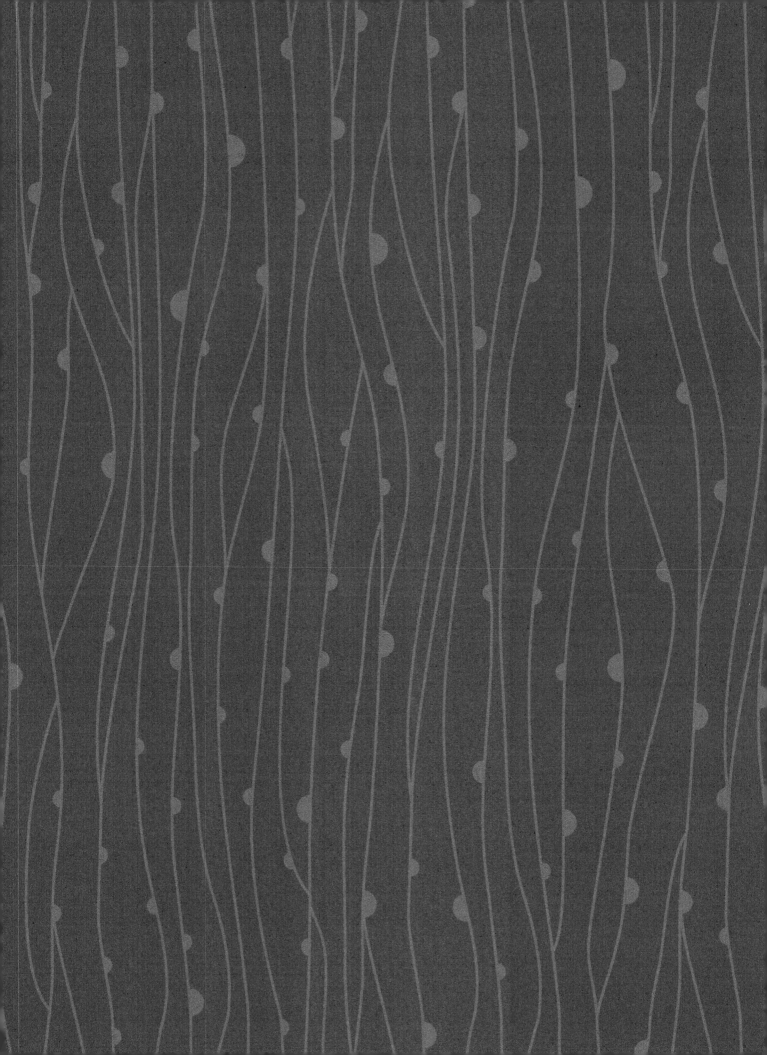

STRAIGHT OUTTA COURT

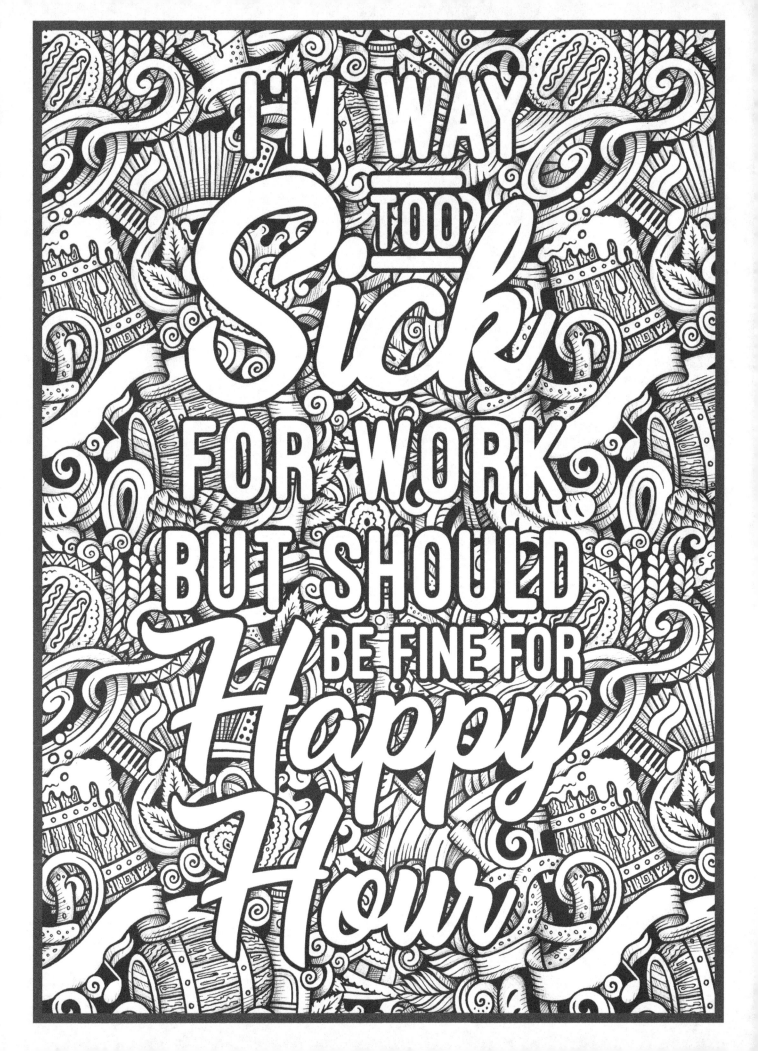

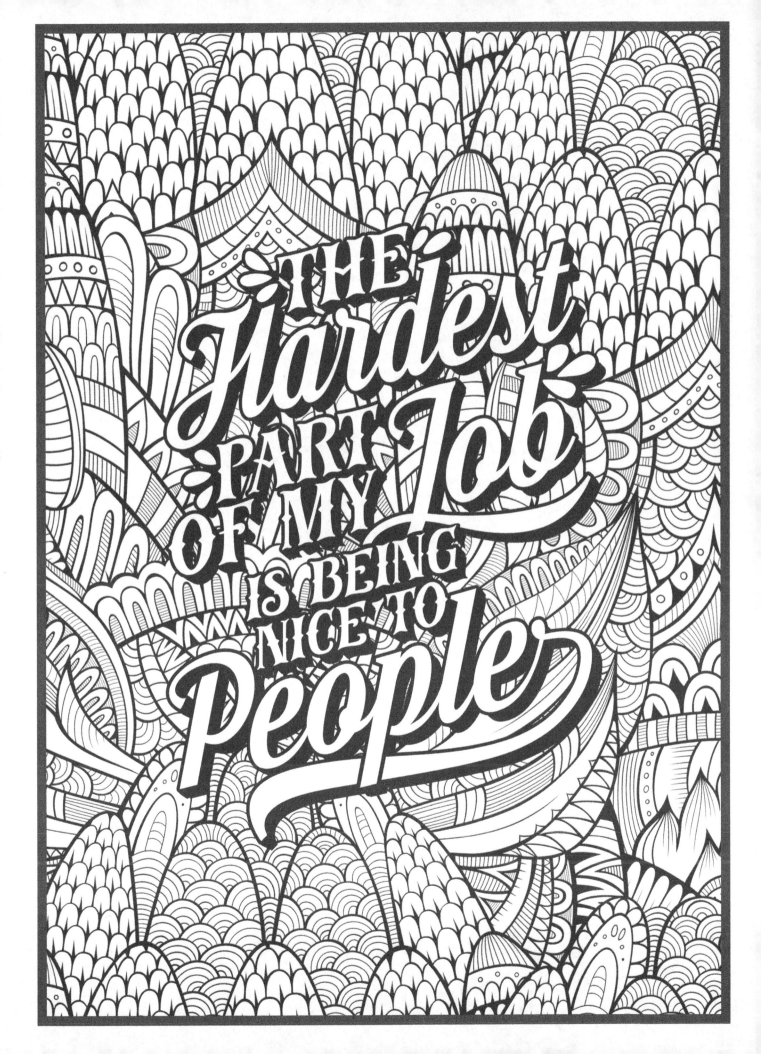

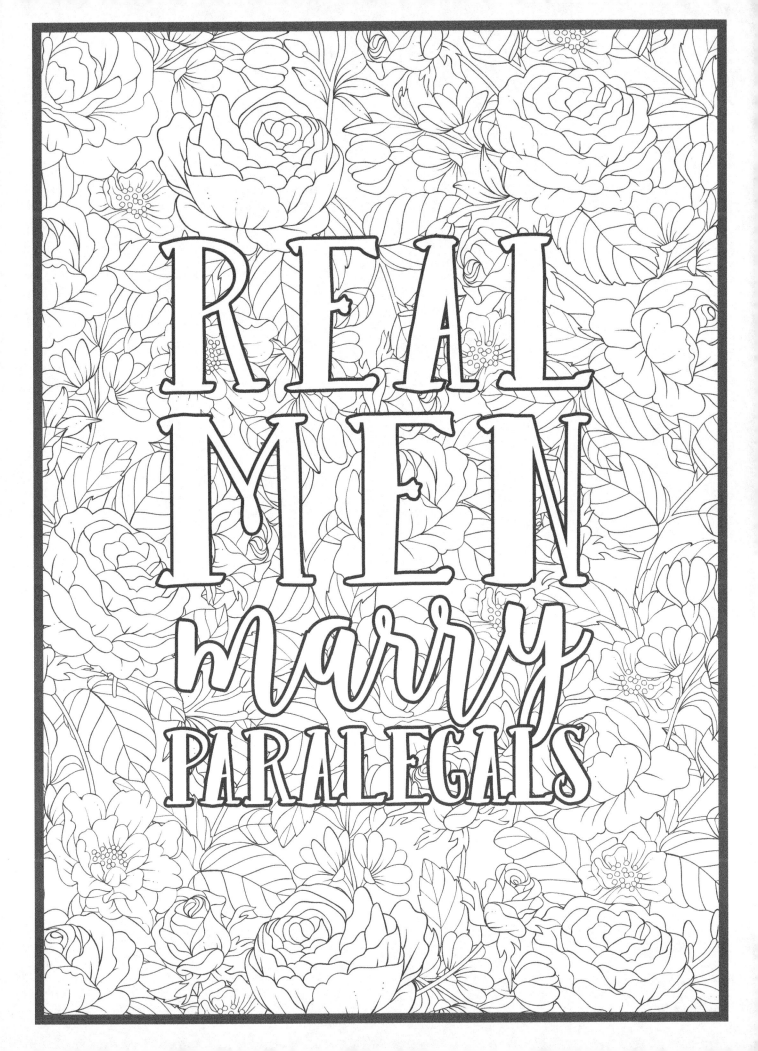

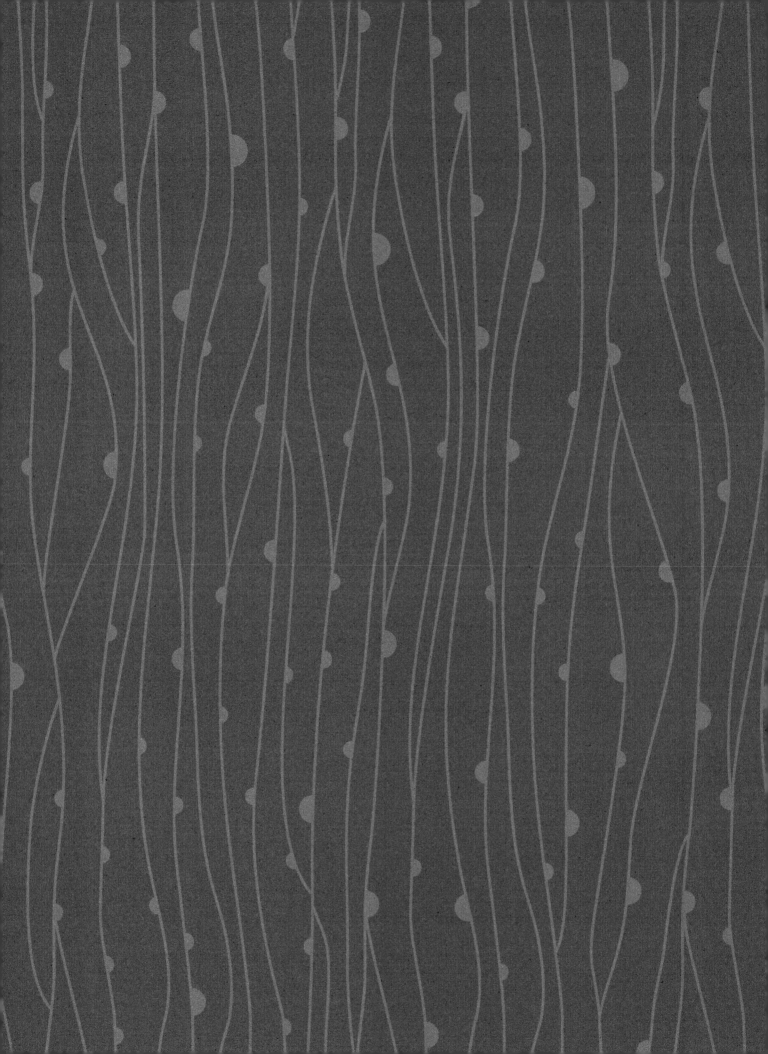

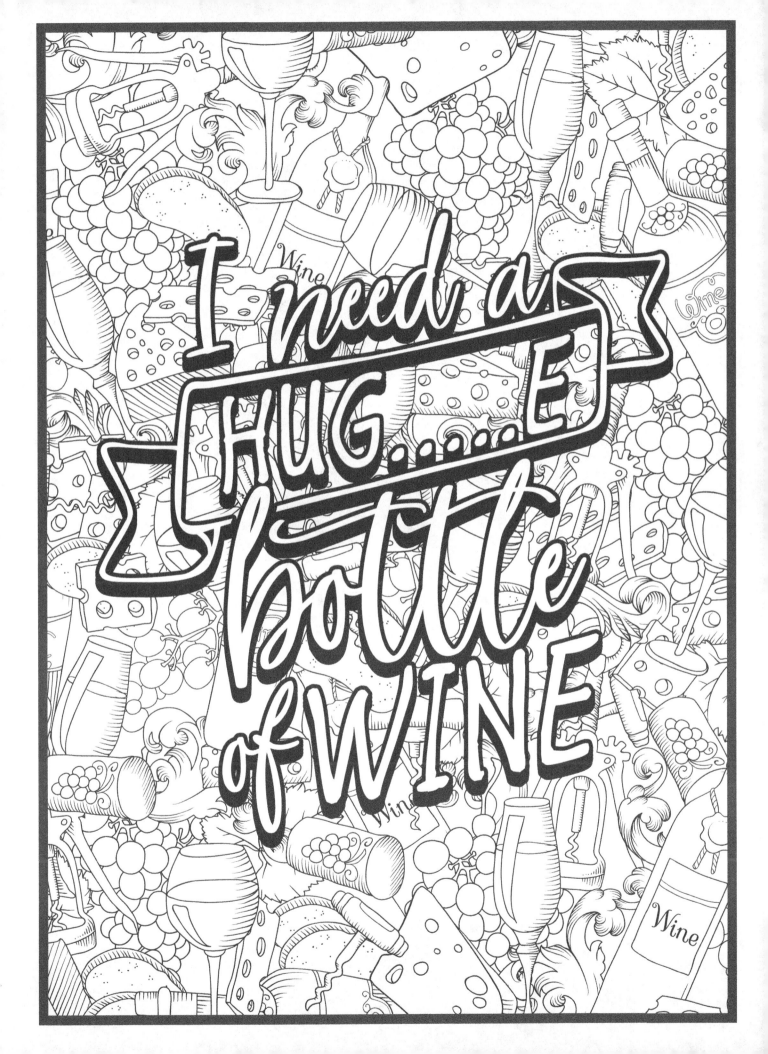

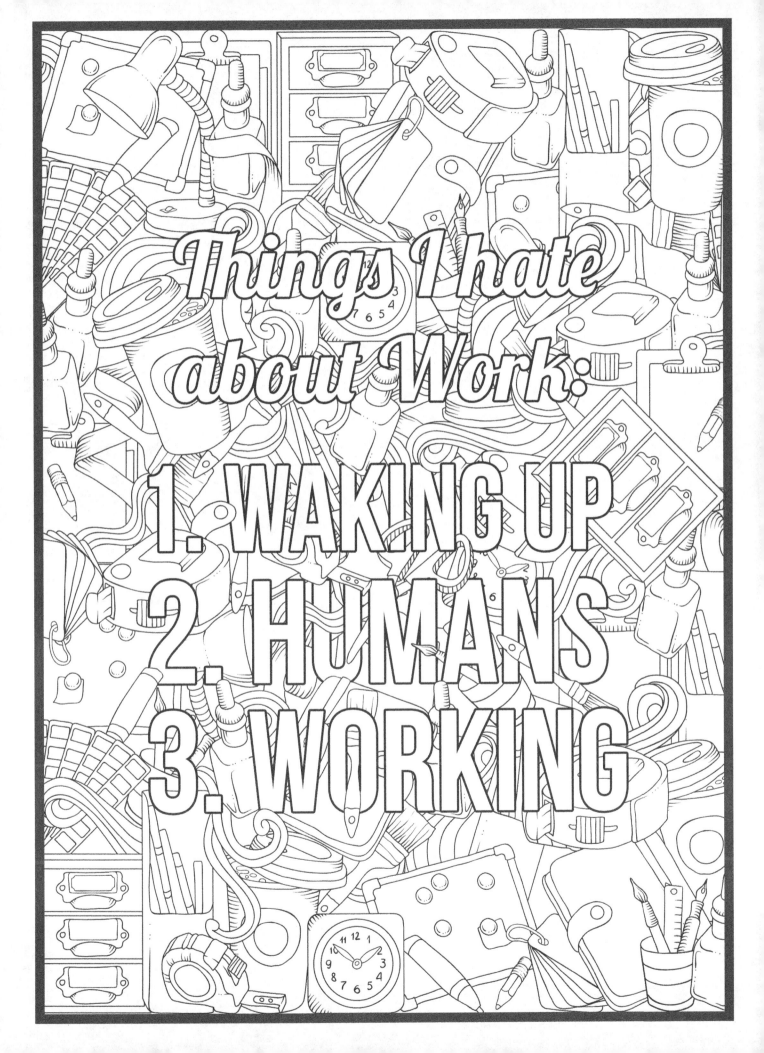

SORRY, BUT YOUR PASSWORD MUST CONTAIN A SYMBOL. A NUMBER. AN UPPERCASE LETTER. A HIEROGLYPH. A HAIKU. and THE BLOOD of a VIRGIN

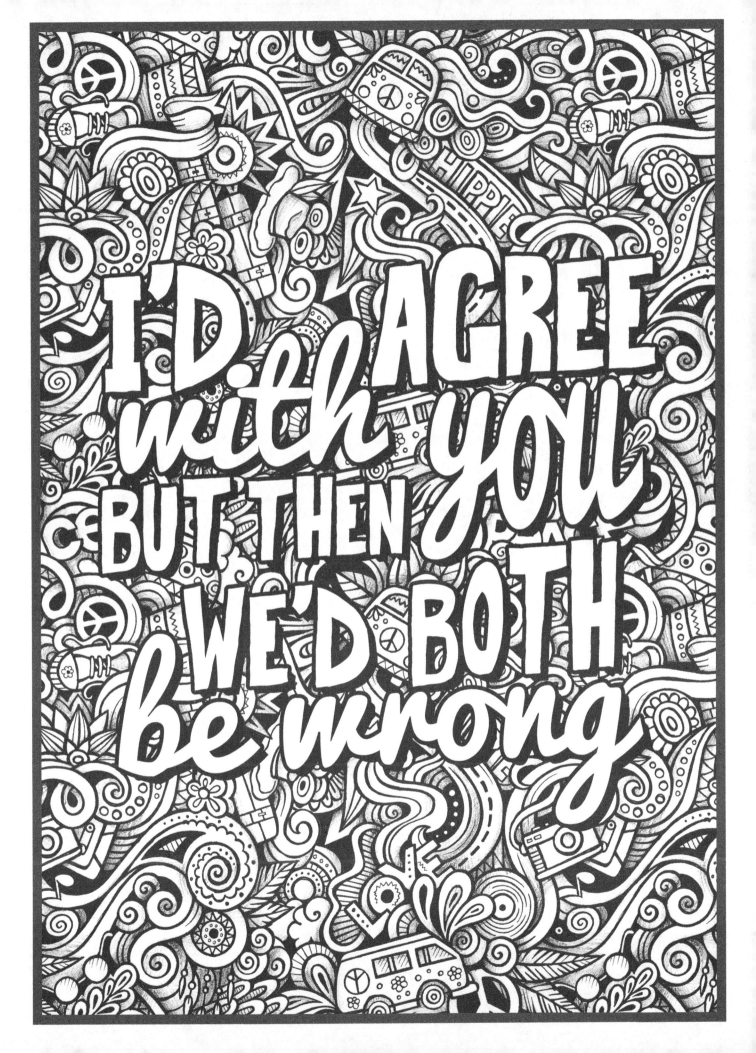

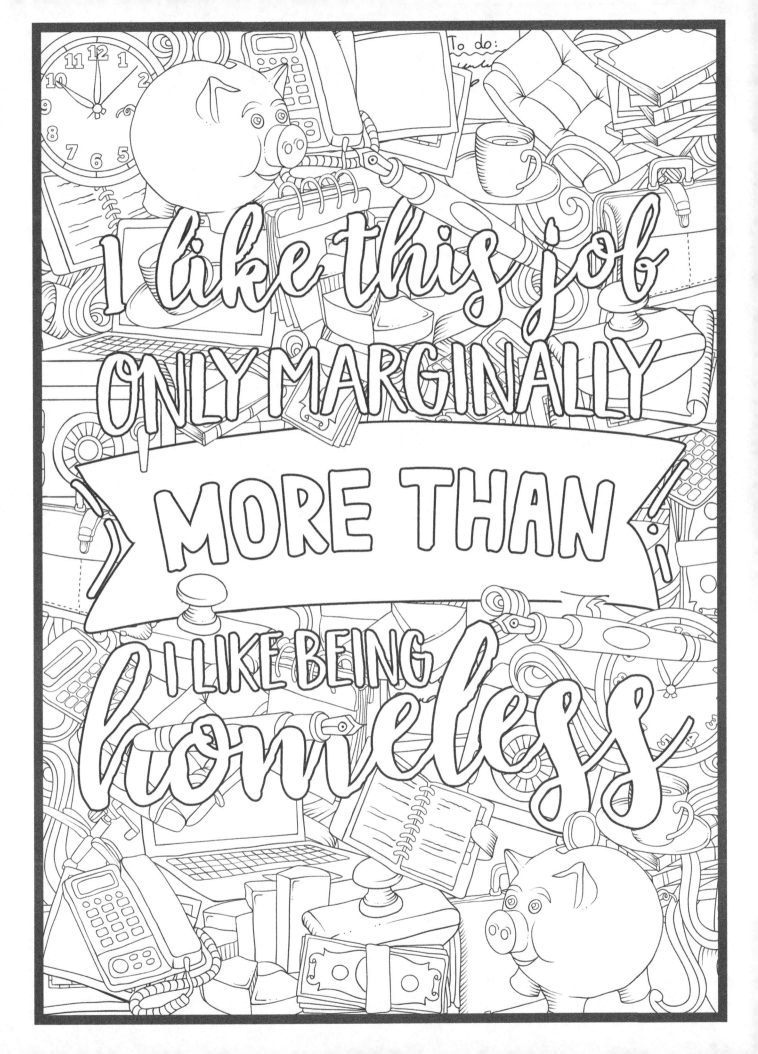

The moment that you REALIZE *that* you've been at work for only an HOUR.

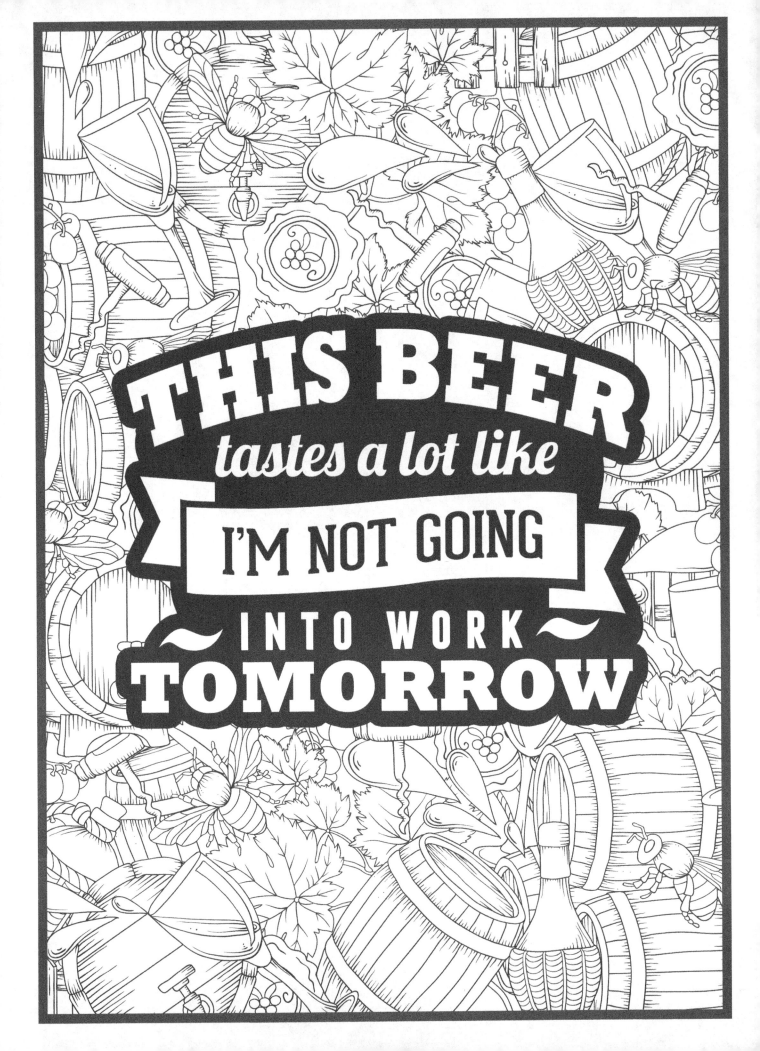

FREEBIE!

JOIN OUR VIP NEWSLETTER AND RECEIVE A FREE DIGITAL DOWNLOAD OF A PRINTABLE PDF <u>ACTIVITY BOOK FOR ADULTS</u> FEATURING INSPIRATIONAL QUOTE COLORING PAGES, MANDALAS, WORD SEARCHES, AND MAZES FOR ADULTS.

SIGN UP HERE

http://freebies.papeteriebleu.com/FRB3

@papeteriebleu

Papeterie Bleu

Shop our other books at
www.pbleu.com

Wholesale distribution through Ingram Content Group
www.ingramcontent.com/publishers/distribution/wholesale

For questions and customer service, email us at
support@pbleu.com